These are the best of rhymes.
These are the worst of rhymes.

Amidst days of stress,
We find foolishness.

By: oldbuck
Merely a rhymester

II

DEDICATION

To all of them:
I want to say thank you for what you just did.
Your reading this book makes me feel like a kid.

You'll soon find I'm no poet, they mostly just rhyme.
Thing's needn't be perfect all of the time.

I don't ask for much money or rich's or fame,
I just like to "make" fun 'cause life's a long game.

So if as you read this you get a big grin,
You laugh or you giggle I'll feel I did win.

For that's the real goal of the time I invest,
A world filled with laughter is the aim of my quest.

So Thanks once again for filling my needs.
It's folks just like you for which my heart bleeds.

~~~~~~

A special note to folks that will find errors.

I apologize in advance for my obvious ignorance.
When they went over punctuation, capitalization
grammar, and spelling in grade school:
This old rhyming fool,
Deserved a "dunce" shaming stool.
'Cause he always made clowning the rule
Instead of listening, way back in grade school.
Think of it as just part of my writing style.
Maybe like an amateur Samuel Clemens. :o)
Thank you. Oldbuck

ACKNOWLEDGMENTS

For all their help on this little book of rhymes, some of it going back many years, I am deeply grateful to the following groups and individuals.

- My family for supporting my rhyming in so many different ways.

- For all those folks through the years, willingly or unknowingly, "Posed for me" as I rhymed my word pictures written here.

- For my Savior Jesus Christ. Who's ministry and finished work have been an often reoccurring theme of my writing from the start.

- For the Holy Spirit's support and encouragement when others weren't able to be there.

- To Calvary Church friends, some have been a sounding board for me a bit over 50 years.

- For all the hundreds of folks that have received pesky emails with lengthy rhymes attached without blocking my name or sending me SPAM.

- To Clement Clarke Moore and his "Twas the Night Before Christmas" for showing me as a small boy, poetry & rhyming could be just for fun.

- To Create Space that made the publishing easier than I ever imagined it could be.

CONTENTS

CONTENTS (CONT)

VI

PREFACE

You are about to read some of the best and worst of 8 years of rhyming by an old retired fella. That is not entirely true. There is worse, much worse. :o)

My hope is that you will find some moments of real enjoyment. However: I'm also aware from " 8 years of rhyming" you aren't going to like all of what you will find here. Maybe none of it.
If that were to happen, I would feel terrible. But I'll never know.

Enough about that.

You will find this little book has been divided into 10 sections. Each trying to give you some idea of the "Main" topic the rhymes are meant to refer to or be about. With any luck at all, they will at least be close. :o)

My biggest worry is the section headed: Dumb & Dumber. They are . . . but I enjoyed writing them and hope you will find some enjoyment in reading them.

Thank you for making the investment and taking the time to read my work. You have no idea what this means to me.

oldbuck, rhymester.

RHYME 1

ONE OF LIFE'S TREASURES

I have something whose "cash" value is of little concern
But its value to me is growing, this is something I learn.

I have a neat treasure. Tiffany is the name.
The halo 'round her face like pure gold, all the same.

The day that we met all wrapped in light blue
With long flowing ribbons the very same hue.

When we first came together I proudly showed her to friends.
Now when they greet us they may think there's no end.

When I turn to her with a questioning look.
She's seldom ever wrong. Reads my mind like a book.

She's so full of energy her hands never stop,
I'm so proud of her my shirt buttons may pop.

We'd been together but a very short time.
I add a gold band. She looks really fine.

But we do part at bedtime it wouldn't be right.
Her face on my pillow by my side through the night.

There's no guarantee how long this will last,
I'm just hoping the future is as good as the past.

The way things are looking we're both in good shape
Maybe we'll go out together in a box that's flag draped.

Now I thank my employer for giving to me.
This neat little watch. The brand ?..... Tiffany.

Written by oldbuck about the 25 yr. watch he received from his employer. The rhyme was written for and read at, an Adult Bible Class Christmas party. Each one had been asked to be prepared to share something about themselves others might not know. This would be the start of my rhyming phase in 2006. 'o)

90 yrs. And Counting
A wrap-up

Some one has said: I can't say the one.
No job is finished till the paperwork is done.

We'll try to sum up the events of that day.
So that years from now no one can say:

Exactly what happened at grandma's big outing.
When they honored her 90 yrs. and still counting.

They all met, as I've said, at home of the daughter.
Lots of folks attended but one less than had aught'er.

Young grandson's at work at a local fast food.
It's hard to reschedule, it depends on their mood.

Well that's pretty good. The families twenty-two.
All with one purpose now this party to view.

It started out great we all grabbed our plates.
All kinds of food and all tasted just great.

Pasta and taters all blended just right.
Enough here for all, we needn't now fight.

The one thing I bit, way more than I should.
Was son in law's pulled pork but I ate all I could.

Baked beans to perfection was part of the feed.
With veggies and berries far more than we need.

After lunch came the photos. The photographers right there.
She lines us all up with such professional care.

It's a high light for me, as I can never remember.
To catch all those shots, of each growing family member.

This way we should get, everyone that was there,
She will sort and re-sort them, with diligent care.

Then ship them by email to each one's PC.
That way we can all see, each one so EZ.

They can print what they want, in the size of their choice.
Or take to some shop, where each will have his own voice.

On just what they want, a few or a lot.
It won't put anyone's budget, now on the spot.

You can keep files for nothing, there's no cheaper than that.
Or fill up a scrapbook with this and with that.

Is it time for the cake. I don't know for sure.
The exact progression, bad memory's no cure.

Well this I remember about that great cake.
The whipping crème frosting, would be hard to fake.

The beautiful frosting is done in deep colors,
Covered with words and real looking flowers.

Dear Grandma it mentions, highlighting her 90 years.
As I opened it, I yelled, 'It says Gloria" to add to their fears.

There's chocolate and white, this cake was made right.
Will satisfy every taste, to the very last bite.

Our son does the honors and scoops the ice cream.
Those flavors together are out of a dream.

We all now get seated, to view the proceedings.
Daughter has it all written, and will do tearful readings.

Of this birthday girl, from far distant past till now.
Things the young wouldn't know, about their pigs and cows.

The years on the farm, all the work and the fun.
The ice and the snow, the bright summer sun.

Folks laughed and they cried as memories pass by.
Some things strike us different, it's hard to know why.

It comes time for opening cards, just look at that stack.
She won't even start, as kids and grandkids, need to get back.

There's a family reunion, on the one mom's side of things.
The kids will be tired, by the end of these two flings.

Our son & his clan have another birthday plan.
To go to a movie and sit in their van.

For one of his younger is now older and is having her day.
Their aim is to celebrate that, in her special way.

One by one folks pack up "take home" cartons of food.
If you leave here hungry, yourself you have screwed.

Like all such events there's things we'd do different.
Myself, the loud mouth, could have been a bit more reverent.

But then, all in all, grandma will be the judge.
From where she sits she's not given to budge.

She likes what went on, food, family and friends.
Sometimes it's the saddest, when if all finally ends.

I'll close this last chapter as I ended the first.
With a wish for the day, an internal "thirst".

I hoped this fine lady would have lots of great stuff.
To think back on daily, living alones kind of ruff.

Well that's not a problem she's said to her girls.
In so many ways her heads just a swirl.

Written by oldbuck, June 23, 2008
As he thought back on the events
from a couple days earlier at the
90th birthday celebration for his
mother-in- law.

RHYME 3
Let's put the 1's In Order

As I now look back, across my whole life.
It's filled with laughs but at times there's been strife.

It would take way too long, to tell everyone.
I've decided here, to tell just some big 1's.

Twas '41 when I arrived. Out of a place of darkness & wet.
Into the light of paradise, I'm not sure I've found it yet.

Those were the days; I'd make my life's start.
Transformed from a child, to a frumpy old . . . fella.

19 & 51, my new baby sister peeks out her head.
It's now just 4 years my "real" dad's been dead.

My mom had moved on, to marry Lem, a great guy.
Who could have guessed, he too would soon die.

Well 61 comes on quickly, I've put school in my past.
I'm at Wilson meat pack but I've a feeling it won't last.

This is one job, of many I will have, but numbers won't matter.
I seem to crave at once, to move on up that ladder.

I try some college and a couple more things.
I'm always ready to move, if the phone would just ring.

In the midst of this time we have a dark cloud.
Our first little daughter is in a white shroud.

She was too tiny, to be on her own.
It scars us forever, deep to the bone.

It's 71, I've just left another, twas selling farmers feed.
A solid item to represent, everyone that I met had a need.

6

But they move you around, all over the place.
It seems any success, is a wild, vicious race.

I jump to return, back to our former hometown.
Thoughts of Nebraska makes both of us frown.

I'm now in dry cleaning. They call me the boss.
That really just means: I'm stuck for all loss.

I'll try direct sales. I'll sell expendable tools.
But the fellows that buy these aren't anyone's fools.

I make the boss a big sale, but it brings no real glory.
It means a bigger sales quota and expands my territory.

I've found I'm a slow learner, I like to be selling.
But travel and long days, begins to be telling.

I'll go to work in the factory. Been fooled way to much
Work in plastics and metal, build switches and such.

It's a good match for me, there's a lot here to learn.
There's just something new, where ever you turn.

Well by now we've by passed, 81's a good year.
All our three youngsters have arrived safely here.

As 91 rolled around, There's' been much to witness.
We've done pretty well, at a little home business.

We made campaign buttons, the kind that tell stories.
We've promoted many groups and shouted their glories.

We moved on from there, to sell wood-n-stuff.
Just to keep it in stock was exciting, but got to be tough.

In just a few years, we were found selling birdseed.
Lots of nice folks, with beautiful yard birds needing FREE feed.

But back at the factory, I still move around.
Up in the wood shop, I soon learn to pound.

It's a great place to work, the leads been there forever,
When they must replace him, will be a major endeavor.

But of all of those jobs, the one I liked best.
Is when I did the teaching, and they don't give a test.

When I'm paid to talk, to folks paid to listen.
Three times a day, catered in free, donuts or chicken.

But that's all in the past, the year is 01.
I've been now retired, frankly missing the fun.

It's cool once a month, to see the old eagle land.
The checks seem small, but take no real plan.

Of course there's free time, 24 times the seven.
But even that's not like being in heaven.

Old friends you once saw, have since moved away.
Have gone to a home, for their life they must stay.

Or some have been taken by cancers and such.
For when you get older, they can't help you much.

Well my life's been reduced, to filling some pages.
You'd think there'd be more, to put out in stages.

To tell a man's story, his life nearly spent.
With just enough money for food and some rent.

Now I'm not complaining, I feel pretty good.
My teeth, back, and knees, ache more than they should.

But that's partly my fault. I just hate the dentist.
And don't use the gym time, insurance has rented.

Well I'm going to close, someone has once said
When you're killing time, don't kid now your head.

For you're dying too, you're being used up.
The end will be nearing and you're no young pup.

Written by oldbuck, with legs to sore, from walking hours at the
fair, to leave the basement and far too many hours on his hands.

Ode to the Traveling Man

Since I've been retired, I'm quite often asked.
My answers the same. Folks can't seem to grasp
My wife and my sister have often commented.
My refusal to travel seems old and demented.

You've got lots of free time, a whole world yet to see.
Out on the road they expect that you'll be.
Well let me now tell you, as best as I can.
Why, as in the past, I'm no traveling man.

It makes no big difference at all where I'm bound.
It seems always to me, there's bugs all around.
As I'm getting older I've grown strong belief.
In knowing real close, there is some relief.

I like to feel always, if I quick get the "call".
There's a place of true rest, just down a near hall
I don't just here mean some cruddy old hole.
But something that's clean, an oft-scrubbed white bowl.

Then when I stop to grab a quick lunch.
I always will question, it's not a wild hunch.
That some things inside or those dark spots out back.
Have things now un-kept. Are lost through the cracks.

I'm sitting here now to soon place my order.
This waiter's accent seems from south of the border.
We can't seem to get past; I'll take just some water.
I want to wait longer till I give my whole order.

To decide, then what's best, what cold drink I'll take.
That's a much later choice, I'm oft prone to make.
Icy sodas are good. Mt. Dews still the best.
But to specify that, makes one out a big pest.

Without the caffeine and a diet drink too.
They then look at me as "Who's fool are you?"
They've only Coke products but just two or three.
But ice cubes and lemon are still served up free.

I'll add a sugar packet, well, now maybe two.
It makes lemonade and saves a buck too.

I just saw the cook, come out of the John.
He was in and out, with his gray apron on.

His hands are dry, there were no clean towels.
I had gone in there first, to relieve my stressed b.........
I remember no towels because when I left.
Bare handed, the door, I had to then heft.

I oft use my wet towel, the door to pull open.
Without one I fear, is a very bad omen.
Of things that will come from this over sight.
The manager hasn't proven, to run his ship tight.

There was no sign in the John. Be sure that you wash.
Before you return, folk's burgers to squash.
To run up and down, that cussed stuck zipper.
Of the hands you had used, do a rinse for the Gipper.

It's a lovely old place, you see through to the kitchen.
The guy chopping lettuce, his nose he's now pickin'.
It's nothing he's spreading, it's probly all right.
It's only an allergy, keeps him up in the night.

They must have decided that silly old codger.
They'll send someone else, to get him to order.
Here comes a young miss that has this strange habit.
Of picking her teeth, I hope she's not rabid.

She'll use those same nails, gripping tightly the rolls.
As I carelessly dropped one, rolled down an arched hole.
For under the table and into the wall.
A tiny small archway. It's not a hard call.

To tell what that's from, there's a cat cross the room.
While leaning above it, a well beaten broom.
I'd say they're on call, used oft for defense.
In case mouse comes out and things get really tense.

There's a bus boy at work, He seems a bright youth.
But with the rag for the table, He scrubs down the booth.
You know. Where we sit. We're from here and there.
And some of the ladies their bottoms near bare.

Where all have been seated on the very same spot.
He's wiping so clean. He's been smoking pot.
I put down some napkins where I rest my arms.
I roll down my sleeves, can't do any harm.

One last look in the kitchen, the guy toasting buns.
Suspiciously thin, down his arms the scars run.
Tracks from a habit, blood tests up to date?
HIV on the increase, these sights I just hate.

Well I certainly enjoyed, my now lovely lunch.
I won't give more details, I'll save you that much.
I'll need to pump gas before I go any farther.
I should now wash my hands but why should I bother.

Remember, no towels, did they choose to offer.
It's all the same hands, you can't rub'em off'er.
The next great adventure, comes just before night.
We find a nice place, to offer our plight.

It's here where my mind, will go nearly crazy.
We'll need wait for our room, the reason seems hazy.
An elderly fellow with a half naked chick.
Come to the desk, drop their key with a click.

Room one twenty four has a very familiar ring.
They hand me my Visa and a very strange thing.
Of course now you've guessed, it's the very same key.
That poorly matched couple have just had a spree.

We'll go by the pool, it looks pretty nice.
But that one scabie kid, appears to have lice.
I had thought maybe later, but to tell you the truth.
That floating on top's, not a mini Babe Ruth.

Up here in our room, they must change the sheets.
But the spread has been on, for days, even weeks.
How many odd couples, of similar worth.
Have claimed this same spot as their afternoon berth.

The carpet is suspect; I'll keep on my shoes.
I don't have foot fungus, I fear, a status I'll lose.
I'm sure that the shower, those stains brown and yellar.
Were caused by the habits of the last fifty fellars.

That don't seem to care, that others will come.
With wives, even children, made to feel they're welcome.
But it saves the guy time, two birds with one stone.
Writes his name on the stall, a skill that he's honed.

As a lad through the years, in banks of white snow.
There are things you must try, it's how young boys grow.
It soon will be the morning; I'll be on my way.
Strange sounds in the night, but what can I say.

It's all part of our travel, it's a crazy adventure.
If you want daily life, stay at home with your dentures.

We're offered free breakfast in a room full of guests.
You now see up close who shared the near nests.

It removes any doubt, about late night sounds.
A couple loud bangs, may have been a loose round.
From guns they're now loading, with scopes and a bow.
They must be wild hunters, from this place I soon go.

I'm back on the road, just four days from home.
I've had so much fun, but worn to the bone.
Maybe if I'm lucky, don't stop quite so often.
I can end this great trip, before I'm found in a coffin.

When I get back home I'll burn my suit cases.
I'll not once again, be put through these paces.
Some folks find delight, in spending their lives.
Out on the highways or parked in strange drives.

But for me, it don't work, I like my small home.
I can walk in the dark and not feel alone.
The drinks in the ice box are all our good kinds.
We don't have to settle as though we wear blinds.

We eat most at home, but when we go out.
We've been there before. I don't sit and pout.
Because of some nonsense I imagine I see.
Most local favorites are as clean as can be.

Well I've spilled my beans the best that I can.
You now really should see, I'm no Travelin' Man.

Written by oldbuck, after a discussion with his sister,
about his reluctance to travel.
She owned and operated a travel agency,
specializing in Senior folk, for many years.

14

The Graduate

Today is your day,
This 25th day of the
Great month of May.

This writer doesn't know you, as well as he should.
He'd just mix some facts up, any way that he could.

To make this rhyme funny, because what he's found,
It's better to laugh, than a face that's all runny.

Recalling sad moments, while vivid and strong,
Need left far behind, to remember is wrong.

On the day you begin a new time in your life
Is no time to bring up, old shadows and strife.

I imagine I'm there, as I look around,
I see few that I know, but your friends, they abound.

They've all come together to show their great pleasure,
You passed all your tests, and now have some leisure.

All here, and they know you, I'm sure would agree
You're a regular "nut", not far from the tree.

You're one of a kind. No one would dispute
You've been "tailor" made, that's why you're so cute.

All are smiling and laughing, the sound seems a blare,
I see your folks in the distance, with big grins, openly share.

Events of your youth with family and others
Great tales and traditions of sisters and brothers.

I don't know your plans, beyond having lunch.
But knowing your kin, tells me this much.

You'll have a great future. Whatever your choice.
I know in debate, you'll have a strong voice.

Cause that's in your genes that wish to make right,
Those things in our culture that form a great blight.

Hang tight to your Jesus whatever you meet,
He'll see you through; you'll land on your feet.

Your folks will tell you, I could go on all day,
But my gift to you is: "That's all that I'll say."

Written by oldbuck as one of our church youth group
graduates from school. There have been many such
youth given similar rhymes they feel compelled to
"graciously" accept.
It's the price they pay for inviting me. :o)

An ode from Grand-dad

I'm an old grandpa,
With grand kids galore.
We've very near a dozen,
At times it seems like more.

When holidays are comin',
It gets their grandma humpin'
Watching her at cookin'
Is really quite "the somethin'"

I always try to save myself
For when they all get here,
I want to be well rested
Be filled up with good cheer.

It's always been real easy,
To say it. . . the wrong thing.
So I make concerted effort,
To limit the pain I bring.

I've long had a reputation
For being mean & gruff.
But their parents would surely tell you
I'm not nearly now, as tough.

On these sweet little urchins
At the ages they are now.
When my kids were kids,
They'd be hitched up to a plow.

They worked from early sun up
Until it would go down.
I know I was the very worst,
Of any dad in town.

17

It seemed I woke up grumpy,
Got worse as day went on.
They probly viewed old dad as,
A very short fused bomb.

But now I've gotten older,
I've learned . . . Well quite a bit.
Something's I've found that happen,
Just ain't always worth a fit.

"Kids will be kids". . . "Relax",
That's what the experts say.
As long as they are theirs,
I wouldn't have it another way.

Lucky for me, each has a phase,
Somewhere 'twixt 3 & 12
Their minds so full of "snoopy"
It's a place I love to delve.

They seem to have good questions
For which I oft' reply.
If at first they won't believe,
Again, I love to try. :o)

For in my mind is fantasy,
I only want to share.
For when I'm gone. . . they're older,
Likely filled with so much care.

For we leave them with a burden,
A curse they must escape.
It's been around forever,
To pick which road, in life to take.

For there is pressure from all sides,
So many ways to easy slip.

As many in sheep's clothing,
Are caught up in devils grip.

If you can't have a little fun,
Before the goin' turns to rough.
For anyone that's been there,
Would tell you times get tough.

So old grumpy loves to kid them,
And make them laugh or smile.
Years later. . . . If I come to mind,
I hope they'll giggle. . .   for a while.

Written by oldbuck, as he pondered the past few days.
All the grandkids and Santa too.
Have filled his heart with gladness and a memory or two.

We built them from air,
Wife and I, what a pair.

A friend had said, to write a nice rhyme.
That tells of my life's assorted pastimes.

There have been two or three, that really stand out.
Businesses you know, about which to shout.

As with most of my rhymes, I must start looking back.
For looking ahead, I have no clear track.

I clearly can tell of things I have done.
While thinking ahead is not always fun.

The past is so vast; it's been my whole life,
Kids, pets, and jobs, and one lovely wife.

Well during those years, I would grow very weary.
Just going to work, seemed often, quite dreary.

I'd get an idea soon lodged in my head.
From something I'd seen, or an ad that I'd read.

That was the case when I started my first.
Bellringer Ad Service would answer that thirst.

I had a busy imagination that ran day and night.
I had some ideas that might work out just right.

I got with a company that really made nothing.
They were in the sole business, of middleman running.

They called this brave venture, Newton Manufacturing.
But the truth really was; they made not a thing.

They simple stepped in with willing salesmen,
Promised to sell, painted pencils and pens.

20

I got signed up at just the right time.
I had price sheets and bags of samples just fine.

My employer and the union would soon be at odds,
For the next several weeks, I could use another job.

But during this time, I saw a small ad
From then, Badge-a-minit, a new product they had.

It was a small button maker, you could hold in your hand.
It was said to make money, if you worked out a good plan.

When it came in the mail, I tried it right out.
I made my first button and let out a shout.

What a great deal, this little hand tool.
I knew at that moment, this business is cool.

I loved to do artwork and selling comes easy.
I'd soon be on top, it sounded so breezy.

With the family involved and many long nights.
We soon had a following, things going just right.

We found great suppliers to grow with this craze.
Credit Unions made loans so easy those days.

We got parts in big barrels and added machines.
We'd soon be filling the pockets, on our denim jeans.

We landed some big ones, The State University,
Back before licenses, became a necessity.

Our single best week. The Hawks and Rose Bowl.
Fans here at home, put our pins on a roll.

Seventeen thousand, four hundred fourteen.
Sold in ten days, a little extreme.

Wife's dad had come down, to see all the fuss.
He ended up making, lots of those buttons for us.

This fun lasted for years, way past now thirteen.
I needed something new, my enthusiasm would wane.

My father in law had worked all his life.
Doing hard custom work and ran a farm with his wife.

Retirement for him, was just a series of days.
He needed new interests, or be fading away.

He bought some small tools and started wood - crafts.
Not wanting to make money, just making folks laugh.

I soon realized, a now growing need.
Across the Midwest, a hunger to feed.

There were hundreds of folks, just like my in - laws.
Wanting to be busy, but had run into flaws.

Wooden parts they all used, would be in demand
Someone local should have them on hand.

I used some experience I'd learned from my pins.
I got good suppliers, would soon start to win.

Parts by the thousands, now filled up the room.
Besides, button makers, had now passed its boom.

We sold off the buttons in two or three years.
We needed more room, we were spinning our gears.

We published a small catalog with hundreds of parts.
The business would flourish, after seeming a slow start.

We were going to move to a home across town.
The business didn't fit, our kids were now grown.

I knew of a crafter who bought tons of our stuff.
I made him an offer, to pass up, would be tough.

They came with a truck, and within a few hours.
All parts made of wood, were now in his powers.

They still run the business, it does well I suppose.
At times I miss meeting all the folks who impose.

When in your home basement, you run a small shop.
Folks always feel welcome and in they may drop.

Well this is enough; I've gone on for hours.
I'd better quit now, it's time for my shower.

One fact still remains, for all of the fun.
I'd never do it again, for there was no real "mun".

Friends by the hundreds, you make through the years.
But most slip away, one of life's greatest fears.

But if you're a youngster, full of spirited unrest,
Maybe running a business, for you would be best.

But know this one thing before you start out.
It's more work than you think, at times you may pout.

The one thing I did, far better than the rest.
For joy and pure pleasure, it passed all the tests.

Was with birdseed delivery, I took to folk's homes.
I have many good friends, while some are real "joners".

Written by oldbuck, after a suggestion by a
friend he revisit some of his
Entrepreneurial experiences.

RHYME 8
Miss Hattie Moves On

*We've suffered a loss
In our neighborhood.
But then at her age
It was to be understood.*

*For she was up there,
In years that's for sure.
And so often for age,
There just ain't any cure.*

*She was past Sweet Sixteen,
My, that's a long life.
But maybe it helped,
She'd never been a cat wife.*

*She'd found a good home,
With the ladies next door.
Whenever you went there,
She was seldom on the floor.*

*She had her favorite spots,
Chairs or other sunny places.
Anywhere she could hide,
From unfamiliar faces.*

*I was one of those faces,
She didn't care for teasin'.
She'd give a low growl,
I'd know I was dis-pleasin'.*

*I loved to tease her,
But always knew in the end.
If it came to blows,
I'd be the one, needin' to mend.*

24

She would venture outside,
Most oft' out in back.
There were other cats there,
But agreed to "not attack".

Because of her years,
And her owner loved her so.
Quite often on a trip,
To the vet she'd need go.

Well, I'm guessing here now,
For the loss of this pet.
They're now flying the flag
At half mast at her vet.

She passed in her sleep,
From reports that I get.
There's no better way,
To pay your life's debt.

Than to reach now the end,
Apart from normal stuff.
To doze off one night,
On your favorite fluff.

Whether she said any prayers,
Or was caught up to date.
She's now in that place,
Where cat prayin's too late.

Try to imagine what it's like,
Only slow running mice.
Huge piles of cat nip pillows,
Warm milk would be nice.

Other cats with like manners,
To play with or ignore.
And lots of time to sleep,
With no one that snores.

Hands come from nowhere,
To scratch ears, and caress.
A regular service,
To clean up a small mess.

That sounds like cat heaven,
That's where she'd go.
For so much of her love,
She's left here below.

But as we now mourn the loss,
We still look ahead.
For who will fill her spot,
At the foot of the bed.

It's a young cat, called Charlie,
Who God sent to now stay.
To fill those girl's leisure,
In those special cat ways.

He won't be the same,
He just never can be.
Another dear Hattie,
There just never will be.

Written by oldbuck, after hearing of the passing
of the neighbor ladies wonderful cat, Hattie.

Our Cat We Call Kitty

We have a feral cat, we call her Kitty.
She's always outside, it seems such a pity.

We were feeding raccoons, out with our bird seed.
When we noticed this cat, had come also to feed.

We feed 3 loaves of bread, from a surplus bread store.
If they cleaned that up, next night we'd leave more.

For now snow was deep, little field mice asleep.
How would this pretty kitty, her health now to keep.

Well this cat had fed itself; she's not the least lazy.
But my wife couldn't stand it; she made her bread and gravy.

We've now even added, a nice fresh milk bowl.
We keep adding more features, to our daily food dole.

The trick now it seems, would prove to be timing.
For if Kitty didn't get here, the raccoons were imbibing.

They loved all the treats my wife lovingly prepared.
One raccoon would come in, if he thought he had dared.

We eat lots of chicken; we like it fixed many ways.
But one thing with chicken, when gone, the bones stay.

Well there seems to be nothing, our gang will like better.
Than a large pile of those bones,They come runnin' to getter.

An entire turkey carcass, we can't believe in one night,
Disappeared from out back, not a scrap now in sight.

We'll our audience has grown, from birds with snack habits.
To 3 big cats, 4 furry raccoons, and "big mama" rabbits.

We buy bags of cracked corn, too keep our birds happy.
But the raccoons like to munch it; they're a little bit sappy.

I'm not sure that a raccoon, gets much energy at all.
But I can't shut them out, that would be a tough call.

So we put it all out, like Bonanza's buffet.
Who's going to get what, is impossible to say.

But at any given time, as I sit in my chair.
There's something outside, Seems to not have a care.

Having their lunch, or just a quick snack.
For later that day, I'll see them scurry back.

The birds start my day, at just about dawn.
A couple times this winter, there'd been a yearling fawn.

But the deer now have grass; we've not seen them in weeks.
And when they are here, with great care, catch a peek.

For they aren't as trusting, as quick birds or stray cats.
Raccoons and rabbits, all sense where we're at.

But I've strayed from my tale, of one little cat.
But that's how it's grown, out on our back mat.

So if you've something hungry, that comes to your door.
Take grandpa's advice, don't run 'cross the floor.

Just keep watching T.V. , or however you pass time.
Don't start bringing out food, or you'll be writing a rhyme.

Written by oldbuck, about the fun they have
feeding wild life on their patio out back.

28

Angus Ain't No Cow.

I've a brand new neighbor,
He's as cute as he can be.
His feet are like shillelaghs,
That's a sign he'll be a tree.

For this fellow is a puppy,
A playful little giant.
But there's no cause for worry,
For this "Saint" will be compliant.

There may be days ahead,
That set his owner near on fire.
Cause this silly little monster,
Loves chewin' on fence wire.

But I know for me it's wonderful,
To have this new found friend.
It's very nice that these young folks,
Are willing, their pet to lend.

For if I find my aging self,
Out lost, in the back yard.
With snow up to my neck,
Finding me won't be too hard.

Just strap a small container,
Of my favorite Mt. Dew.
Around young Angus' collar,
He'll know just what to do.

He'll come straight out to find me,
He'll know my hands not bare.
For I wouldn't come to meet him,
Without Beggin Strips to share. :o)

Well this ends this little story,
But it's not over, not at all.
For as the days grow shorter,
He'll get bigger comes the fall.

So if you find I'm missing,
You don't see my old lawn chair.
Come on round the backyard,
I'll be rompin' with Angus there.

Written by oldbuck after having just met
our neighbor's new St. Bernard puppy,
Angus.

Old buck wrote a bit of an Irish sounding moral
to this next little "Angus" rhyme.

To Our Wives for the New Year.

I know there are those times,
Wives wonder 'bout their man.
Will he ever amount to anything?
Will he ever give me a hand?
Maybe they could learn from this,
They may be trying way too hard.
Just set him on the back step,
Let him get to know the yard.
The next time there's a house chore,
And he's nearly chillin' through.
He may be willing sooner now,
To do some job for you. 'o)

Angus Stays Ahead of the Storm

We have a big dog,
That lives across the yard.
He's a very, very, good dog,
Least he tries so very hard.

With his folks off at work,
This winter duty falls to him.
To clear off all the snow,
So it's easy to get in.

He's evidently found,
If he clears a bit more often.
It makes the job "heart friendly",
Won't put him in a coffin.

He's a bit fussy about his shovel,
He prefers a stout D-handle.
You need to buy a tough one,
Or his big teeth, easily mangle.

You're by now, probly thinking,
It takes years to train a pet.
To shovel off the sidewalks,
Like an old snow plowing "Vet".

But the truth of the matter,
This dog is just a babe.
He's less than one year old,
I swear by "Honest Abe".

I don't know they've done much training.
It's like a kid that learns real fast.
And in no time is doing math,
That's how Angus learned this task.

They left a shovel on the step,
Angus loves to play with sticks.
I'm sure he just grabbed that shovel,
It turns out that's a trick.

He has a size advantage,
Over lots of dogs his age.
My grandkids leave their puppies,
Boxed up, in a comfy cage.

When their parents head for work,
Their little coats are way too thin.
To spend the day outside,
They'd be frozen, tail to chin.

They'd be too small to shovel,
Even though they like the snow.
But they're so short they'd disappear,
If blizzard winds would blow.

But Angus, he's a real big guy,
He weighs 100 pounds, or past.
Those Saints just seem to grow up,
So very, very, fast. 'o)

So when I looked outside today ,
And saw my friend at work.
I just had to save the moment,
Or I'd feel like a big jerk.

Written by oldbuck,
After watching his friend Angus
pushing the red handled snow shovel
up and down the sidewalk as it snowed.

32

Lucky Lance

Hello. . . .My name is Lance,
I've just started a new life.
With an old retired guy,
And his lovely "younger" wife. 'o)

Of course I won't yet know,
How good it will grow be.
But I've got some time left,
I'll just wait here now and see.

So if you ever get to Phoenix.
And you're not there selling drugs.
Just stop by with doggie treats,
I'll see you get some hugs.

But until that happy day,
I'll be catching extra ZZZZ's.
Or playing my little heart out,
How much better could it be.

Your friend, Lance.

Written by oldbuck in response to news, received
from Arizona, of a new dog adopted over the holidays.
Lance. Age 4

Our Lovely Dog Snickers

I was directed today, to a brand new web site.
It's all about pets, and some of their plights.
It got me to thinking, of a dog we once had.
She was part of the family; I felt more like her dad.

When I was at work, one thing I knew sure.
She was waiting for me, her heart was so pure.
When she knew it was time for me to get home.
She'd wait by the door, with a toy or a bone.

She'd have a smile on her face, her tail would be wagging.
Her affection for me never seemed lagging.
If I said, so she'd hear, "I'm taken' the truck."
She always got excited; she hoped she's in luck.

If I went for a walk, she was right by the door.
Looking at me, with her leash on the floor.
Oh she was a shedder, a hair-growing machine.
Our house always needed a thorough vacuuming.

When it came time for bed, she would stand at her cage.
She knew the routine, was as smart as a sage.
Some time a while back, I read of two men.
Who were speaking of Heaven, but of course hadn't been.

One fellow wondered, would they barbecue there?
Will they melt down smores? Could the steaks be grilled rare?
Will they use charcoal briquettes or does propane heat the air?
Would there be a choice of soft drinks or is it just water there?

Will the biscuits be golden? Would they there use some leaven.
They were so filled with queries, about life then in heaven.

Well one of the questions I would ask of those two.
Will my Snickers be there? On my slippers to chew?

Will Heaven be heaven? If that really ain't so.
Is it finally the place where I'll want to go?

Is she still as anxious, to run in the clouds?
Or are things there so different, with men in white shrouds?

I'll not forget how it ended. Then came the conclusion.
Perfection in heaven, is no foggy illusion.

For as my dog had her favorites, chew toys and a chair.
She'll be as happy as ever when her master gets there.

That seems now so clear, that's settled for me.
I have hope and joy, as the end now will be.

If when at the gate, I don't my little dog see.
I'll know I'm in heaven, for my Master will be.

Written by oldbuck, after an afternoon of
thinking about his little Snickers
and their possible "future" together.

Neighbors Make Friends:
Across the back fence.

Each of us have had a friend,
Along the way, one time or another,
A neighbor, or a close co-worker,
A sister or a brother.

Sometimes these friendships,
Take years to catch hold.
At times they come about simply,
Cause one of you was bold.

Well, I saw an example of that,
In my back yard. . . . just today.
I was out romping with Angus,
For how long I couldn't say.

When, Don, our good neighbor,
Called across the fence:
I think I'll bring our Zoey over,
Maybe she'd not be so tense.

If she could rub her little nose,
On Angus' big wet snout.
Maybe then she'd really know,
What that furry mountain's all about.

He brought her by, I grabbed old Kodak,
Hoped I'd get a shot, don't need a bunch..
When Don and Zoey reached the fence,
Old Angus was as pleased as punch.

He jumped up on the fence to greet,
This tiny dog, he'd longed to meet.
As he came up "too close & personal",
Zoey may have felt like "a Frit-o-lay treat".

She could easily have fit in that big mouth,
One small bite is all it'd be.
I'm sure that didn't dawn on Angus,
He just wanted a friend, you see.

He rubbed the fence, and jumped up on,
But little Zoey was looking home.
I guess she may have seen herself,
Buried next to Angus's bone.

We'll not know just how t'would be,
That great big Saint and tiny puppy.
For Don and I are far too old,
To jump into a "dog fight" spree.

We'd need be quick, for with his size,
One bite is all that it would take.
He wouldn't mean to harm the scamp,
He'd only be playing, for goodness sake.

That probly wouldn't matter,
If the little dog were dead.
Don still must go home and tell,
The gal to whom he's wed.

"It was all just in fun",
Who would have ever thought?

The troubles this new friendship,
May suddenly have wrought.

So for now we'll just wonder,
What might have been.
Someday with renewed courage,
We can try it over again.

Written by oldbuck, after spending time in the
back-yard with some friends.
Angus is a near 200 # Saint Bernard.
Zoey is a very small, older, Mexican Chihuahua.
The way the fences are out back, they can't get
within about 20 feet of each other.
They bark back and forth and have always appeared
to want to make friends.
That may still be true, I'm just not sure how we will go
about finding out. :o)

RHYME 15
A Welcome Guest
We call Iris.

When my wife stepped out as she often does.
Fresh morning air, seems to give her a buzz.

She goes out to gather, the printed-daily news.
With its ads and opinions and media views.

Today things were different as she looked around.
Near the edge of the lawn, new colors abound.

It stood a great blossom, just standing alone.
Amidst evergreen bushes and growing in stone.

There slim and tall, with purples and greens,
With a lovely soft look, like rich velveteen.

With petals so fragile, who could defend?
There was really no God, at work way back then.

We were first introduced, by generous friends.
Who offered to share, some bulb odds and ends.

They must be great gardeners, this family from church.
The great kind of friends that don't "leave in a lurch."

They are always quite generous, so this was no change.
Graciously offered the bulbs, without any exchange.

We gladly took them, this one and some more.
We planted them around, t'was really no chore.

The result of that day, as any would say.
Was well worth the time, with nothing to pay.

Here's to a new friend. Twill be lovely to grow.
Rewards have just started for folks that we know.

If these bulbs spread out as we hear they do.
Maybe with others we'll share, not a few.

Unto other green thumbs, an Iris so sweet,
We'll give to some families, a similar treat.

Long years from now, if things keep on ticking.
We'll have Iris galore, for annual picking.

This little rhyme was written by oldbuck,
after his wife pointed out the lovely Iris blossom
on one of the plants given to her by friends
from church, earlier that spring.

Deer's life renewed.

Our next-door neighbors have a deer in their yard.
To figure out why is not very hard.
It's cute as can be, placed tight to a tree.
It stands like a soldier, so proud and so free.

He'd been there for years, he was holding up well.
He's made of concrete, from the street, hard to tell.
Real late in the night, with all sleeping tight.
Some hoodlums came by and spoiled the sight.

They made off with the deer, gone forever we fear.
When suddenly from nowhere, what's the sound that we hear?
There are folks at the door, they have questions to ask.
They have a deer in their yard; to move's a big task.

Before moving him, they wanted to know.
If we knew the owners, that owned him for show.
Of course we replied, our friends from next door.
They'd be tickled pink, and probly even more.

The kind husband and father of the girls that found deer.
Was given the job of lugging him here.
Oh my, what a sight, He's missing an ear,
They've painted him black, permanent damage, I fear.

He was now back at home, but what a sad sight.
Can't ignore that picture; though I try with all my might.
I have some old paints, out in my garage.
Maybe I can use them, Make a nature "collage".

Well my brown is too red; I've no green for the base.
The ear is still missing, from the side of his face.
I can't leave him like that, it's a local disgrace.

Someone found the ear, what wonderful luck.
Now all we need do, to his head, get it stuck.
The owner had gone, and gotten great glue.
She pleads with me, please, what can I do?

I'm up for the task; I've time on my hands.
That deer we'll recover, despite hoodlum bands.
I look the ear over; it's full of small cracks.
It must have then suffered a severely hard smack.

The gorilla and I, That's the name of the glue,
Proceed with the project, to see what we'll do.
Soon four crumbling pieces begin to take form.
We begin to have hope, an ear has been born.

We get it in place, something's still missing.
The top frontal lobe will need some caressing.
Car body filler should make that like new.
While I'm shopping for that, get paints, not a few.

We need tan for the back, Stark white for his chest,
Dark green for the base, would surely be best.
Have I forgotten any? Let's think it through.
Remember black hooves, to make him like new.

Back at the shop, I begin the ear job.
It was certainly easier, when the dopes did the bob.
Thin layers I add, to build and to form.
I'm directed, go slow, or the chemicals get warm.

Then all of the "stuff" will get thin and runny,
The ear will end up, just lookin' real funny.
Victory at last, I do some slight sanding.
Our friend may soon find himself, by his tree standing.

There's only the paint, to now spray in place,
Be careful there now; don't get hooves on his face.
I've gained new respect for folks who then paint.
Those concrete lawn ornaments.
It looks easy . . . it ain't.

Painting and masking, masking and painting.
This goes and it goes, from fumes, I'm near fainting.
My wife stops to view, makes the observation,
With paints, I've made, no attempt at conservation.

The sheer layers in all should keep him standing tall.
Foul weather that comes, winter, summer, and all.
At last, he's now dry, I'm taking him back.
He's looking pretty good, showing nary a crack.

I'm proud of my work, as I look to my neighbors.
I'm proudest of all; I've undone hoodlum's labors.
This probly sounds weird, but he's part of me now.
As he stands his post, I remember just how.

Written by oldbuck after finishing a repair job on a small,
concrete deer ornament from the neighbor's front lawn. It had
been seriously damaged by hoodlums. The elderly neighbor felt
she's lost a friend. I guess I did too.

A few months later he's missing from his spot by the tree,
never to be seen again. ;o(

43

My "Bushy" friend, Harriett

We have a tame squirrel, in our neighborhood.
She's tamed herself better, than we ever could.

I've started to call her, my bushy friend, Harriett.
She's a pretty young thing, hasn't known a Harry yet.

She lives across the street, in a very tall Scotch pine.
I wish it was on this side, in my neighbor's tree or mine.

She's pretty good at looking, both ways before she starts.
But then she stops to play around, I fear she'll lose some parts.

I'm not sure how I would take it, if I saw her flattened there.
With her beautiful red tail, just flappin' in the air.

She's like all silly habits, that in our life we make.
When you're forced to change, it's really hard to take.

She has me trained to sit outside, and wait for her to show.
I'm not sure how that will work, when winter brings the snow.

I click the cup on my chair arm; I "imagine" that lets her know.
I'm waiting there with food; it's time for her to show.

But if I knew the truth of it, I don't really think that's so.
She comes when she feels hungry, whether I would come or go.

Because she knows a waiting list, of eager feeders wait for her.
Each one of us enjoys the show; you can nearly hear her "purr".

She eats right at my feet, Ground peanuts are her treat.
But others feed her various things; She's plenty here to eat.

She'll eat right from your fingers, but I don't do that stuff.
I'm afraid some hooligan, knowing that, could get too rough.

As time has passed this summer, less cautious she reacts.
She doesn't care that visitors, oft come to catch her act.

When she isn't giving us her time, built a nest & raced around.
She's gathered many local nuts, and buried them in the ground.

She can be a pest at times, for she's the boss, no question.
I'm not sure it's good to tame, as I pause now in reflection.

For the more she comes, to be my friend.
The more I'll miss her. . . . . When it ends.

Written by oldbuck, in the fall of 2009 after having been out feeding his little friend, Harriett.

A Side Note: Harriet passed away Feb. 2014 in the midst of one of Iowa's winter storms. It was a sad day for all of us that knew her.

My ugly "grill" friend.

I have an ugly grill but not as ugly as me.
She looks fatally used, as used as can be.

It's spring at my house and time to grill meats.
I go to inspect her and see if she meets.

My great expectations for upcoming feats.
Teaming with me, to grill luscious treats.

She's been on our deck through all kinds of weather.
I should get her a cover but don't know if I'd rather.

Just buy a replacement, every six years or eight.
For this faded Bar-B. That decisions too late.

The old girl is cobbled, though I've not used duct tape
But you might take notice; there are spots where she gapes.

But you laugh when I say; I don't use such a tool.
I knew when I lit her; I'd look like a fool.

The flames shootin' up, from the tape, gettin' higher,
Would surely have caught, my old deck here on fire.

I look the girl over and right at the start.
The hinges seem flimsy, even falling apart.

I'll fix with used bolts, they'll hold really well.
They're an odd shade of rust but you can't really tell.

Cause some scars on the body have caught our attention.
Look post apocalyptic, or should I even mention.

The fact that I've brazed her, that weak, fragile frame.
I used cutting torch gas. Heats all metal the same.

I'd never tried that before, you begin to expect,
It looks kind of sorry, like it might have been wrecked.

Now we've gotten inside, too look at the grate.
It shows now some rust, the wet it can't take.

It's been heated and cooled, a myriad of times,
It seems to be broken, now ain't that just fine?

Well, I'll work around that; I'll use lots of foil,
But that often flares up because of the oil.

Now I'm not discouraged. I'll try lighting her up.
She'll come to life, like a newly born pup.

O.K.

I'll try one more time, she worked fine just last fall.
I've got to succeed, my wife gave the call.

The folks are here now. I can't let them down.
I want to look smart, not dumb, like a clown.

Here grill and I stand, her life nearly spent.
Me, in my soiled apron, I now run out to rent.

A shiny new grill to get through today.
Till I build up the courage, to junk'er, she'll stay.

Written by oldbuck in response to a request
from a good friend for a poem written about "an ugly grill".

Just a note of background. I had a small, not for profit business
delivering birdseed, directly to the homes of elderly folk and shut ins.
It allowed them to buy in larger quantities at a much reduced price.
One of my first "customers" would be the start of a friendship that would last
18 years, until his "final departure" the summer of '14'. One of the many
experiences we shared, was when a newspaper agreed to do an article on
my "Not for profit" business. They needed photos that illustrated my
delivering seed to a customer. Of course Paul was my choice.
The young photographers visit reminded us of 'another' strangers sojourn.
Of course it could just be the "Season" that caused two old fella's a 'senior
moment'. Or possibly the sight of several deer standing in the distant, snow
covered meadow, messed with our minds.
In any event, this is what we remembered of her visit.
With it goes my apology to Clement Moore.
RHYME 19

Twas just a few days before Christmas

A huge digital camera, she had flung on her back
She looked young as a student, at the door with her pack.
With a wink of her eye and a twist of her head
Soon gave us to know we had nothing to dread

Her eyes -- how they twinkled! Her dimples how merry!
Her cheeks were like roses, from the cold, like a cherry!
Her cute little mouth was drawn up like a bow
The long curls on her head, were as black as a crow

She was slim and trim, a right perky little elf
She laughed when we teased her, in spite of herself
She had a broad grin and a very easy smile
We both thought it'd been nice, if she'd stayed for awhile.

She spoke not a word, but went straight to her work
Prepared her big camera; then stood with a jerk
The view finder of course, she held tight to her cheek
The flash it produced will have us blink for a week

48

She took many shots but no film did she need.
Digital photo is grand, yes it's grand indeed.
She knew what she was doing, good photos she'd get.
With two willing subjects, a grinnin', you bet.

Then adjusting her camera again for 'oldbuck'.
After giving a nod, she took a shot of my truck
She sprang to the door, gave to us one last listen.
Then she flew down the drive, like a gal on a mission.

We thought we heard her exclaim as she drove out of sight,
"After a day like today, I'll rest soundly tonight......." :o)

Written by oldbuck at the very start of his rhyming phase.

The "Sale" Across the Street

We have a nice family,
That lives across the street.
They're as good a neighbors,
As you're ever going to meet.

But for the last few days,
Now going on six or eight.
They're holding a big yard sale,
For which many folks can't wait.

It's not because they want to,
Or have a pressing need.
But have an ailing Auntie,
From her stuff, is needing freed.

So this ailing Aunt's sweet sister,
And her daughter, here, the niece.
Have offered up their time,
Each has taken on a piece.

Of this great daunting project,
That's going on right now.
To dispose of all her holdings,
To find buyers, here somehow.

Barnum & Bailey, many years ago,
Put on quite an outdoor show.
Big wagons, tents, & silly clowns,
With wild animals, we well know.

This sale is sort of like that,
Tables, boxes, and tall racks.
As they move it in and out,
I wonder about their backs.

50

For it's not been an easy task,
They've often fought the weather.
With high winds and heavy rain,
They must always work together.

For on a nice bright sunny day,
There's the stuff to now cart out.
They must get discouraged,
But I don't ever see them pout.

Have I mentioned the crowds?
That come racing, car by car.
Most are from real close,
But some come from afar.

This lovely lady's belongings,
Set out now, to be looked over.
Some seem to look so longingly,
Like for a "magic" four leaf clover.

I'll never cease to be amazed,
As I watch each as they go.
They have a look of satisfaction,
They've a bargain now to show.

For each one makes a find,
A "near-new" shirt or socks.
There are dishes, cups, and pans,
A treasured, lovely metal box.

They pay pennies on the dollar,
It's the shopper's constant wish.
All are hoping here to find,
A rare pitcher, vase, or dish.

Like those you see on T.V.
Found at a similar sale.
To make them a shopping star,
Yard sale shoppers now shall "Hail"

But there I sat, just loafing,
In my ratty old lawn chair.
Had been swatting bugs,
And catching some fresh air.

But all of this has me off track,
As this busy time shall pass.
Then I'll be back to watching,
My growing weeds and grass.

Written by oldbuck, after spending time
watching the neighbors efforts
to dispose of their Aunt's excess personal
belongings to help fund her stay
at the care center.

52

An ode to our gym trainer.

There's a new gym in town. It's called Lively Wheezers.
Families want champions, made from bent over geezers.

First time we tried these workouts, we felt we were brave.
But were winded in minutes and soon felt like a slave.

We were frightened at first but have now peace of mind.
We are at ease 'cause we know, our leader cares and is kind.

We join in with real gusto, she leads with no fuss.
At our gym we have someone, trained to show us.

How to be active and strong, past a hundred and two.
She will only ask of us, what she knows we can do.

No matter the member, old farts or their chicks.
She does what it takes, to see it all clicks.

It's not always easy, the sound grows too loud.
The music she plays, may not suit every crowd.

But she takes it in stride, this good little soldier.
At times when she must, she can get even bolder.

She doesn't ask much: Sign in, bring some water.
Count when she counts, and breathe when ya aught'er.

Grab a chair, weights, and bands, we'll use every one.
You'll also need a ball, before your time is done.

Marching in place to warm up the core.
She's up front through it all, our leaders no bore.

Drink lots'a water, set your pace, work out smart.
Cardio's good for your heart but keep checkin' the chart.

Now it's triceps and biceps and give me four more.
But no jumping jacks now, those ya should'a done before.
When we've finished stretchin', deep breathin' and are cool.
She always has kind words or may say: "Now hit the pool."

When the session has ended what surprise is in store?
Will it be prizes or baked goodies? She brings offerings galore.

We have one who understands our aches and our pain.
She wishes everyday each one shows her some gain.

All the time we'll be tryin' to show appreciation.
For all the effort and concern, she's been demonstratin'.

Not because it's her job, to smile till she glows.
But she loves her work and can't help that it shows.

Written by oldbuck after his retirement, he spent some time at a
local gym and had a great leader.

RHYME 22
An Old Fat Man's Lament

The weeks from autumn leaves, to winters white snow
Halloween, then Thanksgiving, it's soon Christmas you know.

The grandson's trick or treat bags sat around here for weeks,
Sweet tarts & Snicker bars, and a chocolate smell that reeks.

I wouldn't buy all that stuff but it came here for free,
Those folks paid good money, I can't waste it you see.

Then comes that big day I'm so thankful for
I eat till it's gone, no matter how much, I never eat more.

It was sweet "tatters" with brown sugar and huge turkey legs
Lots of green beans, cranberries, and a dozen deviled eggs.

And then the full week, we call Christmas round here,
Candy canes, stuffed dates, and egg nog for good cheer.

There's the Planters mixed nuts from my mother-in-law
I gobble those down, like a bear with five paws.

It's hard to resist all the treats and good eats
I've put on heavy layers, from my neck to my feet.

But it's a New Year now and time to make promises
This year I'll slim down, I've just pledged to the Mrs.

I'll cut back on eating or grazing it's called
I'm not a big eater, just some ham & cheese ball.

A good little snack to hold me till dinner
But I do want to get healthy and look a lot thinner.

There's a gym down the street, a place I call torture.
Insurance pays the bill, "Just go there" is all they ask for.

Must view as a great thing 'cause some claims they don't pay
It guards against falls, diabetes, and heart attacks they say.

I went for six months, six months ago now,
But when I look for my feet, I'm back as fat as a cow.

I've not got the stamina or balance I had
Six months with no work out, it really is sad.

How quickly it leaves us, when we turn our backs
I must get goin'; I'll find a sweatshirt and pair of light slacks.

I'll look in the closet, away in the back
My gym shoes are there, deep under the stack.

Karren got me a great water bottle, at a Health store at the mall
She said I could use it, when for cool drinks they oft call.

Well as I've taken time now and given great thought
It's more fun to write poems than to do what I ought.

Maybe I'll start out slow, I've been flexing my fingers
At this keyboard for hours, but I seem prone to linger.

My neck is so stiff, and I've pain in my back
I pretend that it's worth it, as a computer "rhyme hack".

But maybe sending this lament to family and friends
It will motivate me, to do the right thing in the end.

Written by oldbuck as he contemplated going back to the gym

56

RHYME 23
Nurse Julie

We all have some places we'd rather not go.
When it's our turn, we often walk slow.

You know those places, where they press and they poke.
They ask personal questions and needles are no joke.

Yes, Doctors and Dentists would form a short list.
Of places I don't like, prefer I could miss.

But there is a bright spot, when I've ache or pain.
There's one that's there, helps me come back again.

It's our Doctor's, Nurse Julie. She makes it O.K.
She always is so helpful, in so many thoughtful ways.

She answers our questions and helps work us in.
We always feel "it's urgent", when ailments kick in.

But it's not only what she does, some of that's just her job.
But the manner she does it, she's never a blob.

She's a smile on her face, she never seems down.
As a matter of fact, I've not seen her frown.

She lights up the place, with the way that she is.
I'm sure all her patients, agree she's a whiz.

Well that's all I know, about this good lady.
I trust Doc knows it too, treats her real good on pay day :o)

Written by oldbuck, after his daughter reminded him of what a
great nurse our family doctor has up front. Of course her name
has been changed to protect her privacy.

Older Timers, Drivers lament

I'd like to beg you, Yet today if I dare
Always and ever, Please drive with great care,

For it's me on the highways and byways you share
I'm that poky old fellow with gray in my hair.

But I've finally retired and I think that it's fair
To ask you sometimes, Your horn not to blare.

It don't mean much to you, You really can't care
You're in a great hurry, A lunch you may share.

But when I see how young drive, I often despair
For the life you might save, Is the one that you bear.

Oldbuck

I've included this short rhyme on the outside chance someone
might read it and heed it.

Old folks understand, everyone doesn't have the "spare time"
that we have but unfortunately; sometimes younger folk don't
appreciate that old fool is doing the best they can to hurry.

Many elderly are forced to drive past their prime because there is
no other affordable way, to get to doctors visits or the store.

Maybe of some younger person would occasionally offer an
elderly person a ride, it could save them both time
and even lives.

Thank you for your consideration. :o)

Floods of 2008 and Beyond

The weatherman says: " The Cedar will rise."
The numbers now sound like into the sky.

It's not long ago, the year 93.
It came toward the house, but stopped at that tree.

Well we better do something, we don't know for sure.
How high it will get, the levies no cure.

Now comes the first flood of neighbors and friends.
They all band together. Sand bags they now blend.

Into huge, endless snakes, around homes and yards.
That's held it before, as they stand silent guards.

There's an air of excitement. I won't call it fun.
But we'll fight this together, we won't ever run.

We move stuff upstairs, onto tables and chairs.
It should be safe now, at least calms our fears.

But T. V. keeps saying, it's worse than they thought.
The rains to the north, more feet they have wrought.

It's rising here now, it creeps cross the yard.
We must go to a shelter, but leaving is hard.

We pray that they're wrong, it can't get that high.
I'll be out of work, with no money to buy.

Even simple, everyday things, much less a new furnace.
Oh calm yourself now, that old river won't hurt us.

It's now in the basement, that won't be so bad.
Of course it's a mess, and we're not at all glad.

But neighbors have had worse, we feel rest assured.
There's life past the clean up, least that's what we've heard.

It just keeps on rising; it's up on the porch.
If it keeps on coming, all we'll need is a torch.

We sit at the shelter, now in a great haze.
It seems like forever, but only four days.

They tell us a notice, Great FEMA will send.
They seem to control, everything from that end.

They'll do some inspections. Leave stickers on doors.
The color will tell "safety", not really much more.

They talk about buy-outs, demolish or repair.
Some say they don't care, they seem filled with despair.

We have family around us, they promise they'll help.
They're all working stiffs, they won't yip or yelp.

We've been notified: we pull on our boots,
We're anxious to get home and back to our roots.

We've got on our T shirts, our gloves and our mask.
We look like a ragged army, but feel up to the task.

The next flood now comes, it's one of emotion.
As we climb the porch steps, to get clean-up in motion.

We stand at the door. Tears run down our faces.
This will be a big challenge, but we've won other races.

We'll get beyond this, it will all come together.
It would help us a little, if we got some cool weather.

Everything goes to the curb; I can't believe what I'm seeing.
Our entire life, now past us is fleeing.

It's all covered with a mud, a horrible thing.
I can't find the box, where we stored our class rings.

All the things we worked hard for, raised as high as we could.
But the walls and the ceiling, are soaked to the wood.

The works moving along, our friends have been great.
I can't begin to describe, the good meals that we've ate.

But another floods coming, it's a non-ending rumor.
Some are so wild, they border on humor.

But there's no one laughing, no one that I know.
Can believe the reality, of what's beginning to show.

Uncertainty is king. Wait is the word for today.
Good questions get asked, but no one can say.

Exactly what's next? Can we get our permits?
Can we get on with life, or must we live as hermits.

For now I've no facts, to add to this story.
We're still filled with hope, so "to God be the glory".

Time heals all wounds, they say in the end.
For now all we need, Is for God to now send.

A miracle our way, for just some clean beds.
A comfortable place, to lay weary heads.

We don't ask that much, a small simple place.
A place to call home, our lives to then face.

But I look to the future: I see memory floods.
On birthdays, anniversaries, it's just in my blood.

When my boy is in college, I won't have, to look back.
Any pictures of him, not even a short stack.

There will never be now, our old wedding pictures.
Or Auntie Ruthie's tarnished, aging lamp fixture.

All that funny old stuff, each family socks away.
To pull out on occasion, so each one there can say.

"I remember it well, the day was so sunny.
And old Uncle George was acting so funny".

But today is the day, we now must get through.
We're bound to get stronger, if we don't break in two.

There's just one thing I'd ask, when you read this rhyme.
It could now be long years, and the passing of time.

Has dulled the shear horror, of those fateful days.
But for those that live on, we'll remember..... always.

Written by oldbuck
This is a rhyming "collage" of media articles from the last several
weeks woven together as a single story. As family & friends
continue the seemingly endless cleanup process and the
struggle to get on with their lives.
Their goal is; " just back to normal".

Our TV Weatherman
Loves Winter's Snow

Our weatherman's got a smile,
That goes from ear to ear,
When he can say: "There's snow",
"It's deep and coming here".

The leaves are all most gone,
One day left of curbside pickup.
But as I look out my widow,
They are too frozen to rake up.

In our city of "5 Seasons",
Fall has surely fallen.
It snowed yesterday
It's now cold as a Valhallan.*

But that's "par for the course",
Which too have now closed.
I guess most later golfers
Would be feeling too "exposed".

Many "birds" have gone south,
Some long weeks ago.
A few wait thru the holidays,
Too see a Christmas snow.

But there are still a few,
Of we hardy Iowa folks,
That snowbirds no doubt,
Will oft' make their "corny" jokes.

We sense hints of laughter,
That accompany their pics,
Of sandy beaches at sunset,
With tan bathers just for kicks.

We've pulled out our fleece,
Dusted off, tall winter boots.
It may seem silly to some,
But this routine is, imbedded in my roots.

We gas up our blowers,
Make test runs 'cross the lawn.
Dig out gloves & stocking caps,
Warm coats will keep us "thawin".

I'd like to show a photo,
I just snapped out the back.
This scene is soon covered,
By scores of "beasty" tracks.

We've got bird feed in stock,
There are also cat snacks.
But hopefully no cat treats,
Will be our birds out back.

I'll just grin and bear it,
As I boil water for hot tea,
I bet some of those old snow birds,
Are quite jealous of me.

Because it's in their blood,
They can't seem to believe.
The cold is really healthy,
From mosquitoes will relieve.

Well I'll bring this to an end.
I've things that must be done.
There's some chili to finish up,
With a steamy burger on a bun.

Written by oldbuck, as it begins to snow again.
The 3rd time in as many days. :o)

- - - - - - - - - - - - - - - - -

*The *Valhallan Ice Warriors* are the Imperial Guard
Regiments from the Ice world of Valhalla.

RHYME 27
Winter Weary

A rhyme that sends a winters "chill'.
With snow, not knowing where to start.
But as he's had some time to "chill".
A fellow with a changing heart.

~ ~ ~ ~ ~ ~ ~ ~ ~ ~ ~ ~ ~

I've never been one, for heading down south.
As soon as the leaves, Get as dry as a drought.
They hang there all golden, all orange and red.
I think of all the song birds, they must be "winter" fed.

To pack all my stuff, in the back of the car.
Head then for the border, always seemed. . . going too far.
For me, I suck it up, buy warm socks & shoes.
Turn on the T.V. set, grab snacks and Mt. Dew's.

Ball games, there are many, furnace has been checked.
There are plenty of groceries, pantries piled. . .double decked.
Why this great rush to join the 'grey haired' masses.
That will take their big R.V.'s to the Florida grasses.

To the dryer called Arizona. To the spaces called Texas.
You wimps are spoiled. What you need are more taxes. :o)
Those were yesterday's thoughts; I've had them for years.
I think all my adult life, since dry behind my ears.

But since Global Warming has hit the Mid West.
Maybe heading down south, might really be best.
You see, for a month, it's snowed and now blowin'.
The temps are so low, they're barely now showin'.

The numbers are all negative, wind makes them worse.
I have words for all this, but not fit for a verse.

I've just come back inside from attacking tall drifts.
So if I seem a bit upset, I'll admit that I'm miffed.

I cleared my double drive to get our cars in and out,
Then the plow comes along, that sight makes me pout.
All the snow from up the street is now piled in the hole.
At the end of my driveway, makes me feel like a mole.

Always digging out, just trying to keep ahead.
All this talk of Five Seasons, I've for years been mislead.
The extra season was to enjoy, least that's what I'd read.
I find it's merely time, for more winter time instead.

Seems I've gone on long enough, I'm starting to thaw.
My hands are warming up, yes; they're still rough and raw.
But my jeans are near dry, there's some feeling in my feet.
I suppose it's not too late, to go back to the street.

To make one last pass, to clear those big drifts.
I'm glad we've had this chat; my mind's "clearly" made a shift.
Yes, it's now 8 below, the winds out of the North.
The drifts in my yard now move back and forth.

But the snow is so pretty, as it hangs from the trees.
No snowflakes are alike, as they shift with the 'breeze'.
As I look out the back, the feral cats have been down.
That black one, so frisky, so playful. . is really a clown.

I couldn't be serious, about leaving all this.
So I'll send you old snow birds, my great winters wish.

Where ever you are, midst the sand and the bugs.
I'll stay comfy right here, wrapped in blankets and rugs.
I'll eat lots of the wife's chili, navy beans with great ham.
Her piping hot biscuits, smothered with P.B. and jam.

There's beef soup w/ fresh veggies, all diced up just fine.
With fresh homemade noodles. A salad . . cheese but no wine.

I know it sounds strange, this quick turnaround.
But I'd miss the challenge, keeping both feet on the ground.
When you're fighting the ice as it piles on the walks.
They insist if you don't clear it, city fathers will squawk.

I'll not worry about that, in the spring there's no snow.
When the grass is getting greener, spring flowers then show.
I'll be here to see it.   Iowa. . Then at her best.
I'm lucky to be here . . . . I feel really blessed.

Written by oldbuck, after spending several hours today,
playing in the snow.

RHYME 28
My Dad Was Just a Lad.

I'd like to share my story,
Of a young man and his wife.
They were my mom & dad,
And would be all my life. 'o)

Their family lives to tell this tale,
As thousands more, relay the same.
Because we must repeat them still,
So no one thinks. . . War is a game.

* * * * *

Their story seems so common,
Of a "40's" married life.
Couples lived from day to day,
Fearing soon he'd risk his life.

Daily papers filled with horror,
For those were darkened days.
Everywhere were vivid tales,
Folks killed in terrible ways.

Then as though right next door,
Japan attacks our homeland.
Our President came on the air,
Said: "For this we cannot stand."

So now, this young family man,
Must drop what he was doing.
Leave wife and kids to fend alone,
To go where troubles brewing.

They said: Good-byes, a kiss, a hug,
Those last few hours went too fast.

Not wanting now, to let them go,
For these moments may be their last.

O'er those months some letters came,
Our Sailors, on a ship at sea,
He wrote he was a "water tender",
We weren't sure what that could be.

He was on a brand new ship,
The USS Horace Bass,
The KEEL was laid in '44
APD would be her class.

With a crew of over 200 strong,
But for most, their first time out.
In the weeks and months ahead,
They'd learn what "WAR" is all about.

Headed out for the great Pacific,
Okinawa, at Hagushi anchorage.
371 Enemy planes shot down,
As our Fleet would vent her rage.

Then came those grueling days,
They called this duty, "picket line".
The enemy must cross this space,
But heavy shelling is what they'd find.

There were occasional escort trips,
To Guam and then Saipan.
It broke the tension of daily fire,
Which was fine with every man.

Returning from such an escort trip,
A submarine blip came on the sonar.
8 depth charges would be dropped,
Watch for oil slicks, on open water.

History was made April 25,
Bass had sunk a mid-size sub.
The only APD to, "git'er done".
36 enemy, "sank" inside that tub.

It was the night of July 3 0,
Things were seeming very still.
When they heard the cough & sputter,
Of a crippled plane, out for the kill.

It caught them really by surprise,
Flying in darkness, fast and low.
Headed straight now toward the Bass,
Wanting to take its fatal blow.

The very last moment before impact,
That killer plane went o'er the side.
An aerial wire had caught his wheel,
Missing our ship, that "kamikaze" died.

One American killed, 3 badly injured,
More injured slight, but still could fight.
The Bass puts into Buckner Bay,
Ship & injured were soon made right.

They would be among the first,
Task Force 31 would find their way.
To take position way up front,
To occupy their Tokyo Bay.

August 27, at 0810, Captain Flynn,
It's official: Nagato admits defeat.
The last lone fighting battleship,
Of their Great Nipponese fleet.

Well now I pause to catch my breath,
Our young man will soon be home.
As thousands more hit U.S. soil,
So many of them, will feel "alone."

Families were there, that's true,
And friends, now by the score.
But they had not seen the suffering,
The deaths, and so much more.

* * * * *

12 Jun 1945 With Japanese troops hopelessly surrounded in the
Oroku sector of Okinawa, Japan requested a ceasefire to allow
them to commit suicide rather than surrender. Hundreds blew
themselves up with grenades or jumped off cliffs.
22 Jun 1945 The Americans secured Okinawa, Japan. Three
months of savage fighting had cost the Japanese 129,700
military and 42,000 civilian dead. Just over 10,000 were taken
prisoner. The Japanese also lost 7,800 aircraft and six capital
ships.
The Americans had lost 12,520 dead, 36,600 wounded, 763
aircraft destroyed and 40 warships sunk.(Historical estimates)

* * * * *

I'll close with just this "added" tale,
Of this "Old Veteran's" rhyme.
To share how one man's story,
Ended. . . way before it's time.

He went back home to Iowa,
Packed up the wife and kiddies.
He and his kin, adventure bound,
Were on their way to the Windy City.

He and his brother had a plan,
Build trailer homes, of wood & steel.
To help young families, make a fresh start,
A place a couple, "at home" may feel.

As their "dream" took shape,
Soon past, expectations grew.
The brothers bought some man toys,
Cars, boats & planes, but just a few.

"These are the days, They'll never end"
Is the song a young heart sings.
But as comes to all, our life is done,
The day our death toll rings.

He was killed one fateful day, 11/47,
His Piper Cub, his pride and joy.
Had done that trick a dozen times,
A turn of fate, for our young boy.
* * * * *

These are recurring thoughts,
I find rushing through my head.
When I think of all our veterans,
Both the living. . . and the dead.

All the lives now represented,
In rows of many snow white crosses.
In graveyards round the globe,
That mark our American losses.

Courageous men and women,
Willing to sacrifice it all.
Americans still answer, now as then,
Their "HOME" countries, urgent call.

With Deepest Love & Great Respect,
I sign off now, *"**Wish you all the best**"*
We remember you for what you did,
And how you all, have passed the test.

* * * * *

Written by oldbuck, In recognition of the sacrifice of
All our Veterans and their families.

* * * * * * * * * * * *

The story is of his father,
And the brave fighting crew of the
* * * USS Horace A. Bass * * *

Richard W. Buck WT3/c(T)
SV6 USNR
Honorably Discharged
1/21/46

RHYME 29
An Itsy Bitsy Spider ?

I think I have a spider,
That's living right down stairs,
As I've often seen it hanging
By its sturdy, homespun hair.

It drops down from the ceiling,
It drifts from side to side.
If I take a swing at it,
It really takes a ride.

It's not so much I mind,
She's a tiny little thing.
But if she caught me napping,
Would her little bite then sting?

The past few days and nights,
I've had some "itchy" bites.
I don't know what they're from,
Be it spiders, flies, or mites.

It's said there are some bed bugs,
Been found in small motels.
But I've not been to one of those,
It's been now quite a spell.

I've done my "bug bite" research,
It seems they think its ants.
Or maybe little jiggers,
That crawl up in your pants.

I do spend time outside,
Just loafing in my chair.
And more than once I've swatted,
My arms,.. My legs,.. My hair.

But in the past, they had a name,
If we whined then to our "mums".
Whenever there were itchy spots,
Folks simply said: "No See Ums"

Nail polish and old Calamine,
Were favorites in my day.
You never saw a Doctor,
Cause for that you'd have to pay.

I guess today's no different,
Except now I'd catch the bill.
For common stuff like this,
There probly ain't no pill.

For now I'll just keep scratching,
Adding ointments where I can.
It's just some itsy bitsy bug,
I must face it like a man.

So I've written now this rhyme,
To get this itching off my mind,
Scratching annoying bug bites
On my ankle, and . . . . behind. 'o)

Written by oldbuck,
down in the cool basement
on a "Steamy" Sunday afternoon

An Ode to:
The Last Christmas Goose

I'll tell this sad story, but twill be a short tale.
Because as a goose, we have only short tails.

I'll tell you a story about a great goose.
The story of course is of me on the loose.

I'm just starting to tell this, when my life's almost over.
It won't be too long; I'll be pushing up clover.

It wasn't always this way, me teary and sad.
There once was a time I laughed and was glad.

Those were the days; I thought they'd not end.
Now I find myself victim, for myself I must fend.

When I was part of the flock, things seemed a lot better.
I was not standing out, more like "birds of a feather."

There must have been a dozen, good healthy, fat birds,
We all were good friends. Seldom shared a harsh word.

But that too would change, as our numbers grew thin.
You had to be quick if you wanted to win.

Win what? You would ask: that's the troublesome part,
It brings up the farmer and the knife to our heart.

You see the whole value of geese on a farm,
Is not too look pretty or to poop in the barn.

No, we're wanted game when winter comes round.
Out comes the small hatchet. Leaves a head on the ground.

One by one they were taken, to a place we don't talk.
To a stump in the back, where the last go to squawk.

Thanksgiving is coming; I'll make it past that
But I'm on extra feed, it's making me fat.

I'll get very worried, as Santa draws near,
That's the time of year so many geese fear.

So what's the big deal? I say with a shout
I've looked all around and see no geese about.

That can mean just one thing; my days are now short.
Unless I make to the farmer some clever retort.

What do you say to a fella that follows old habits?
No ham or roast beef or gray furry rabbits.

Adorn the man's table at this time of year.
Nothings better than goose, with their Christmas cheer.

So let's say: Good-bye. It's been good ta know ya.
If I had more time, I'd love to have shown ya.

All over the farm, the in's and the outs.
But now little buddy, I've just time to pout.

Say farewell to the others, as you learn their names.
If they seem out of sorts, remember....... farmer's game.

Written by oldbuck after his older daughter kidded him about sounding like another well known rhymer, and should write a silly goose rhyme.

Some get away.
An ode to small bears.

A walk in the woods
Can be a great treat
Keep an eye out for honey
We all like to eat

It's me and my brother
But mom leads the pack
She says that's in case
Wild dogs would attack

We're dressed all in black
Just like all our kin
Folks when they see us
Say: "it's our little bear skin"

We've tiny little claws
That soon grow to be tools
For digging and clawing
We bears are no fools

We soon learn the ropes
That's what our mom hopes
Her plan never was
To raise silly cub dopes

She struggles sometimes
Too keep us on task
We like to goof off
"Keep up and don't sass"

Just follow her lead
Is all that she asks
We soon, in the sun
Would like to just bask

But that's when it happens.
A visitor, mom sees
We'll have some fun
We just love to tease

Of'times it's a hiker
Or biker we see
Some, lost in the woods
As scared as can be

We don't mean to seem rough
We're really just curious
Sometimes folks get mean
Try to sound rather furious

Some take a bold stand
Throw rocks or kick dirt
They don't understand
It don't really hurt

Most head for the hills
Some climb up a tree
We guess that's because
It's just better to see

But here's all we want
Just leave all your stuff
We seldom eat you
One treat is enough

A good illustration
Just happened last week
We came on a fella
We snuck up for a peek

We were right up behind him
He seemed in a daze
When suddenly he sensed us
Turned around for a gaze

You should have seen
The look on his face
He spun back around
Feet started to race

Mom lumbered along
At quite a safe distance
Brother and I might need
Some assistance

To open his pack
Too look for some prize
He couldn't care less
Had big saucers for eyes

He was forming a plan
By now he was tiring
Oh what he could do
To avoid just expiring

Out there, far from home
With no others around
It made sense to him
To get up off the ground

The very next tree
Would be his escape
He shinnied right up
Just his knee took a scrape.

Well there, he had made it
Safe at long last
But he didn't realize
Mom had a question to ask

She'd reach up the tree
To gain his attention
He started to scream
"Just what's your intention?"

"What is it you want?
"I've left all my stuff
"I've nothing here now"
"Isn't that quite enough?"

Mom asked just as calm
As bears can speak up
"My kids wanted cookies
Or cream in a cup"

"They like sugar cubes
Ripe apples, or fish
Or a big old bee hive
Full of honey's their wish"

Well, he wouldn't speak up
So we spread out his stuff
From his back pack and duffle
Prob'ly seemed kind of ruff

But that's what we do
On a day in the woods
When a camper won't openly
Share all his goods

So here's some advice
You can take it or not
If you're out in the woods
With bears at your spot

Just say what you've got
You needn't add strife
You may even go home
With more than your life

Well, mom says I've gone on
Too long, but that's normal
One thing I would add
My shiny black coat........
is really quite formal

oldbuck wrote this after receiving a wonderful,
picture of a moose antler carving, of a bear family,
from his sister in AZ.

CAUTION
This isn't meant to be a serious recommendation for
handling "real" bears. It's just a silly story.
Wild Bears are no joke. Please explain this to any
children that may be reading this. Thank you.

RHYME 32
Why did the Chicken
Cross the road?

Some say this truth, we'll never know.
The facts won't ever, clearly show.

Why a chicken, One day so happy.
Would suddenly do something so sappy.

To step out on that busy street.
With her often slow, yes, stumbling feet.

To start a dangerous journey, one bad as it can be.
It couldn't be as simple, as to see what she would see.

Could it be that dear old farmer, got over come by greed,
Failed to give our chicken, the feed that she would need.

He'd still want eggs, each day come out.
She lets him down, He'll hoot and shout.

We know where chickens end, when laying's getting slow.
They go in cooking pots, with noodles down below.

Or maybe she decided, to try her wings at last.
Her feathers may be growing, really, really, fast.

Did she stop to think it through, that in the street could die?
If she finally took the chance, and found she couldn't fly.

It could be something odd, No one would ever guess,
Have you seen a mama duck, with ducklings on a quest?

She may have seen them, a waddling down the road,
Completely unaware, a truck's a heavy load.

84

She may have thought, that looks like fun.
They only waddle, they never run.

I'll go myself, on one quick trip, 'Cross this road I live beside,
See for myself at last, what that distance always hides.

We're never told just how it ended.
There's an outside chance, we'd be offended.

For there's seldom mention, beyond that day.
Of what that chicken, had to say.

The moral here. I think there's one.
Think it all through, before your next run.

Plan your trip well, each move out complete.
Before you set foot, out there on the street.

Written by old buck, after considering various notions
on why "the chicken crossed the road".

A glimpse at "A" retirement.

I worked over 45 years for somebody else
So finally, one day, I could retire.
I dreamed of sleeping in late
Just watching TV by the fire.

I dreamed of leaving the pressure
All the politics and such.
I never dreamed I'd miss the folks
From work, so very much.

Wife dreamed of long vacations
Enjoy seeing hill and dale.
But unless you're made of money
Some of that's a fairy tale.

I junked my safety glasses and my badge,
The old work shoes that cramped my toes.
But the rest of my plan, had a mind of its own
This is how, it so often goes

My wife had also been thinking
Had some good plans of her own.
She saw lots of time, with tiny grand kids
But alas, they've all gone and grown.

I went out of the birdseed business
So I wouldn't have that daily chore.
Now I watch my T.V. till really late at night
But still find, I'm awake before four.

We oft go to the gym on Monday
That afternoon I mow the lawn.
Early on Tuesday, we're back at the gym.
In the p.m. I'm eagerly trimmin' that lawn.

By Wednesday, maybe a medical need
Wife may have a query, or I order more pills for me.
Some friends are getting replacements
Will my aching hip be next, or my knee.

Dental appointments on Thursday
Or is it a.m. eye glasses to start.
Friday we may have prescriptions to fill.
Or just while away time at Wal-mart.

Early Saturday, wife's off to market
With a list of items, she's gonna' get.
We really don't eat that much
But someone's still got'ta fetch it.

No one plans their kids might return
Bring the grand son and their dog along.
It's been some over a year now,
Their own place is where they belong.

It's great to have the grandson,
Attending a good local school
We pray God is working, to help find them a place.
It don't need to be fancy or have an indoor pool.

When we make the trek, to near West Des Moines
Mostly highway driving, but one minor speed trap.
To visit son's growing family, count'em, now there's 8.
It's a 4 hour visit with 4 hours time on the map.

One of the things no one mentions
We can't take any overnight trips.
I can't see to drive after sunset.
That's one of my "old age" rips.

Restroom confusion may someday
Keep us from Church quite so much.
We'll both really hate that, I know.
But you count more on timing, than luck.

There's nothing wrong with the restroom
I can't always recall where they're at.
I'm reachin' that point with my bladder
I'll need that route down really pat.

We don't often need to plan next week
Just be sure one of us can still drive.
Can't forget where the Docs and clinics are
We may need them, just to survive.

So don't build your plans to high my friends
While putting your time card in its pocket.
This may be a typical retirement week,
May be here before you expect it.

oldbuck

Don't Envy a Silly Rhymer

Someone recently wrote, as they finished a rhyme,
"I long to do rhymin' myself here sometime."
"I wish to put down, clever words on a line,
My thoughts there so clear and stated so fine."

Well let me tell you, as one who oft rhymes,
It's more of a curse, than blessing at times.
For it builds up pressure, for wanting to share,
Unfortunately when done, few then seem to care.

It's more like a belch that builds up its steam,
So few then approve, or so it would seem.
For whether the cause was for lyric appeal,
Or a wonderfully filling, home-cooked meal.

The outcome's the same, from those now exposed,
They're wishing you were . . . . A bit more reposed.
Just keep it internal. Do not with us share,
This creative outburst, into our open air.

Just keep it too yourself, no matter the cause,
Linger. . . think it through, take time now to pause.
For whether its rhymes or belch's you've shared,
As I've said here today so few will have cared.

So if it's just some relief, you're longing for,
Just kick off your shoes, and lie on the floor.
Patting your tummy and taking deep breathes,
May make you feel better. . . . relieve that distress.

For once it's released, there's no getting it back,
I've done it so often, I've long since lost track.
But it comes to mind now, as I finish up here,
The thought of a truth, I've grown to hold dear.

It makes me feel humble or even just simple,
How even a cheek, without trying, can dimple.
Or the face of a teen can produce a big zit,
Why rhymes for so many are not a great hit.

For if you had many monkeys, long rows of typewriters,
Give them enough time, to go along and not fight'er.
A troupe of untrained, might eventually produce,
Some of Shakespeare, or now famous, Dr. Seuss.

So you see my dear friend, for now your delight,
Might really soon show you, it really aint' right.
To take now your free time, or burn the night oil,
For when you are done, You may have wasted your toil.

Written by oldbuck, after receiving
an email from a fellow that said he "envied" anyone
that could write rhymes.

- Repose is: dignified calmness

It's 'Nothing' to Rhyme About.

I'm leaving the drive, headed where I don't know
I've got a few bucks I'd be willing to blow.

On two little girls, they are my grand daughters
I tease them so much, way more than I aught'er.

They love to attend to all kinds of green plants
They love all of nature, even skeeters and ants.

I bought some small flowers, thought I had old some pots.
I looked high and low but find them, could not.

So I'm off to my hardware. They've a big garden center
Just for green thumbs. That sounds like a winner.

I'm stumbling around and who should appear
But a friend from the gym. It's our leader, I fear.

She leads the old gray hairs as they move about
She makes it more fun, as they sing and they shout.

They keep time to loud music and move with the beat
I used to do it but nearly died from the heat. :o)

She hits me up hard: "Where have you been?"
I said;" Just taken' it easy, but should start up again".

She tries to be kind, she spots my big belly
And see's when I laugh , it's a bowl of "fat" jelly.

We visit a while and speak of old friends
Some names I remember, have come to their ends.

Well, they went down trying, to stay in good shape
For some it works wonders but for some it's too late.

Well, we're both out on missions, she's looking for lots
Me and the girlies still need those clay pots.

We part with a wave, and a promise to send
Some more of my rhymers, she'll read to the end.

I soon find the clay pots but they're red as can be
I'll paint them snow white, they'll be easier to see.

Maybe I can "Picasso" a picture or two
To help them sort out, which one goes to who.

I escape the cashier for less than 5 dollars
I don't really care, though I'm tighter, than a dress shirt collar.

I don't think it matters to those little tikes
It's the thought that still counts, ain't promised them bikes.

I get home at last, to mix up my paint
It's going O.K. but an artist, I ain't.

I'll wait till the morning to add the cute stuff
I find painting wet paint can be kind of tough.

Well, I've gone on forever reporting my trip.
I've never really learned, to keep my lips zipped.

The moral of this story has just got to be:
If you see it's me coming, keep away and stay free.

If it's obviously me, out loose on the street
Turn quickly away, pretend we don't meet.

Or you may be trapped too long at the store
I'm often gone longer, oft forget what it's for.

Oldbuck wrote this in response to his Aunt's observation
that he could write a poem about 'nothing'.

This is a rhyme I wrote just for
my favorite Aunt Shirley. :O)
RHYME 36

Surely, it's hard to be humble.

Surely, it's hard to be humble
We're so perfect in every way.
We can't wait to look in the mirror
'cause we get better looking each day

To know us is to love us
We are one heck of a pair.
Surely, it's hard to be humble
We're doing so good, it really ain't fair.

We're used to oft getting' noticed
Most others just can't near compete
They're merely attention starved strangers
that we meet . . . out there on the street.

We could probably find better comp'ny
but for now, we've got what we've got.
Who cares? We'll never get lonely
As long as we're prouder than snot.

Why surely, it's hard to be humble
When "you're perfect" is easy to say.
We can't help but look over our shoulder
'cause folks are always lookin' our way.

To know us is to covet,
We've got so much, we really could share.
So surely, it's hard to be humble
And sadly, we don't really care.

I guess some could say that we're loners
Iowan's, old, tough, and proud
We'd have lots a stuff if we wanted
but couldn't stand the sad, jealous crowd

Folks say we're "egotistical"
we don't know what that even means.
But guess it has something to do
with the way that, we flew past our teens.

You know it's hard to be humble
when you're perfect in every way.
But can't wait to look in the frig
'cause we're hungry most all of the day.

Just to meet us, is to love us
That's been the way with old Bucks.
Surely, it's hard to be humble
when others don't share our good luck.

Aunt Shirley, I'll close with this comment
I'm sure your thinkin' it's true,
"My nephews so good with his poems,"
With envy your turnin' bright blue. :o)

Written by oldbuck for his favorite Aunt Shirley.
She is my dad's youngest sister and about my age.
We always have fun when we are together.

This Too Shall Soon Be Past

As I sat here, eyes on the TV set,
I had started, near to pout.
For the temps are well below zero,
To go out, I'd freeze my snout.

Is this the way, I'd spend my day,
Just idly; wasting away.
For if you're killing time,
You're dying too, they say.

Then it crossed my mind,
The time it passes fast.
We'll find with this New Year,
This Too Shall Soon Be Past.

For its January twenty first,
One 12th the year soon past.
Maybe I've been spending,
Too much time "repast".

For next to all the hours,
I find myself in bed.
I pride myself in this,
I've always been well fed.

However: I'd made a resolution,
To make an effort all year thru.
To write more rhymes each week,
And pass them on too you. 'o)

For your simple, self-enjoyment,
Or you may critique a few.
Then if you know a lonely soul,
You can stuff their email too. :o)

I'll try to head them up,
With a subject line that hints.
A rhyme here, you've just opened,
I'll write plainly and not mince.

On the chance it doesn't ring a bell,
Or sets your mind a tingle.
Just delete now the "spam",
No longer will it mingle.

It won't break my heart,
For I'll never really know.
The very thing that if I knew,
Might cause a lethal blow.

So if today, you've read this far,
You know it wasn't necessary.
But if we meet out on the street,
Try not to act the least contrary.

Cause we're still friends,
Through thick and thin.
You'll just likely never know,
Where that day I've been.

For most my silly rhymes,
Tell of some day's simple story.
Of today or days gone by,
Some are light and some are gory.

But often too, I hope's the case,
They share another mighty win,
Of Jesus precious blood,
O'er Satan's world of sin.

So with these rhyming words of wisdom,
I've shared here, all that's new.
I'll return now to my TV set,
And wait to hear from you. :o)

Written by oldbuck, as he huddled inside,
with outside temperatures well below Zero.
It's difficult to have an exciting life adventure,
wrapped in a blanket ,
watching T.V.in the basement.

Good-Bye My Friend

It must have been a tragic day,
When Sara Jo, found her friend.
Who would have guessed?
Her life so young, would so early end.

But there she was, just lying there.
An old pill bottle, beside her chair.
Her eyes were closed, as though asleep,
Seemed now at Peace, without a care.

They ran some tests,
It's just cop's habit.
They took some blood,
To inject a rabbit.

But there's no lab test,
Can prove a troubled mind.
Only a tear stained note,
So often left behind.

Good-Bye My Friend,
Is all it said.
As Sara Joe had stood. . . . . .
And very calmly read.

I care for you so much,
No one could ever know.
But miss my Little Lamb,
This act will surely show.

This note of sorrow,
Of sadness grown.

They were so close,
Should she have known?

Sara would this note,
Take to her grave.
From Mary's fragile Mother,
This great grief might save.

But it seemed to all, Mary had committed,
This one last act, of desperation.
To somehow now repay the Lamb,
To make to some, a declaration.

For years ago, she had stood by,
As "Little Lamb" was sure to die.
Divided up in roasts and chops,
With parts to serve as kidney pie.

A prideful papa, had made his point,
For on that day, t'was he who bossed.
As she and Lamb's sweet friendship. . . trust,
Would be for years, forever lost.

But in her heart, frail Mary knew,
That little lamb she'd not forget.
I trust this thought, to be her last,
That they today, in Heaven met.

Written by oldbuck,
After thinking on the "possible" details of Mary's untimely death
declared in a note to Sara Joseph Hale, the young lady that would forever
memorialize Mary & The Little Lamb.
This is a very "dark side" of a children's jingle,
I have written to give "possible" details of the accounts of that fateful day,
Mary's lamb went to school. The entire story, some 20 or so pages, is so
dark, I will never publish it, but thought this might give others something to
consider without all the details of the entire tale.

Where do Rhymes Come From, Anyway?

Rhymes are thought strange, most love'm or hate'm.
Groups come together, Just to debate'm.

To jump from a rhyme, into a real poem.
There's all kinds of rules, I don't want to know'em.

There is not in my head any notion of changing.
Or even improving, these words I'm arranging.

For me it's a method, to share with a few.
A piece of my mind, as older I grew.

An old retired guy, with time on my hands.
I sit in the basement, in front of big fans.

It's a hot summer's day with nothing to do.
Then, seems out of nowhere, some rhyming words flew.

So I'll put them together and make up a rhyme.
Sometimes it goes fast, while others take time.

It takes no real topic to get me, here started.
I hear a bird sing or the dog may have …barked

It seems like some magic or maybe a curse.
I jump on the keyboard to record a short verse.

I really do know, most never get read.
But that very thought, seldom enters my head.

I've done it so often I never think twice.
But once to be read, would be really nice.

I love to rhyme words; most sound they're ad-libbed.
Some try to be funny, like a poke in the rib.

Some are more pensive, more serious and calm.
I'd like to think those, might serve as a balm.

To heal, heady wounds; to help with your past.
But I know they're just words, and probly won't last.

I have no great goal, to teach or to train.
But rather a wish, to just entertain.

I don't weigh my words, I just rattle away.
You can rest well assured; your mind won't be swayed.

We "fools" have a volume, of words we must use.
We may try your patience, But don't mean to abuse.

They're all filled with love, though some may not seem it.
If I've lived a bad life, Now's my time to redeem it.

But that's a new topic, and seems kind of heavy.
If I let it get started, It may just go on and on and   :o)

Written by oldbuck, as an explanation,
for rhymes that folks take to enjoy reading.
Well, they are willing to take anyway. :o)

I've Got Good News,
Sad News and
Great News.

A long, long time ago,
Out there in a place,
That we no longer find.
Is the start of Human race.

God chose to call it Eden,
It was a perfect garden.
Living in such a place,
Your heart should never harden.

God had made this place,
For Adam & for Eve.
It was so filled with love,
They couldn't then believe.

What God had said about a tree.
That He had placed in there.
With lots of luscious hanging fruit
But they were not to share.

For this was like a "magic" fruit
Like nothing come before.
Eating just one bite of this,
You'd know the final score.

You'd suddenly be smarter then
You'll see & know God's fear.
That man would have this, "Knowledge"
That we'd hold fast and dear.

Their Temptation

The story starts with Eve and Sin
"Old Sin" was a snake she knew.
As they talked together,
Her "snoopy" quickly grew.

Old Sin assured her, then as now,
"Real dyin' can't be true."
"That's not the sort of thing,
Your Loving God would do. "

Adam came to see the fuss
When he heard, he couldn't stop.
Cause ever since, the saying goes.
Idle hands are Sin's work shop.

Their "Original" Sin

Well Eve had waited long enough
She took a bite, it's not that bad.
Old Adam too, could not resist
From here on out, the stories sad.

Suddenly from out of sight
God's strong voice was callin'.
This young pair and all to come
By their choice, had fallen.

Adam said to his young mate
"We've parts God can't abide."
God agreed and offered each,
A generous animal's hide.

For they had failed their only test
God always said: "Enjoy the rest."
"Cause if you slip and take a bite,
You'll both become, to me a pest."

"You thought of me,
I won't be tough,
I'll soon forget,
You'd call my bluff."

"But that's not so, I can't forget,
It's going to get now really rough"

Their Fall From Grace.

So from the garden,
They were, in shame, lead out.
To work and toil and sweat
To forever mourn and pout.

It's always been like that
Since that time and hence.
Man must work to have,
Shelter, barns, and fence.

But there's some good,
Has come from this.
God sent His only Son
So if you truly wish.

And if you're willing,
Him : to trust and serve.
Christ will forever after,
Your "washed" soul preserve.

Believe & Repent

So turn your back,
Now from the snake.
For he's the one,
Your heart will take.

He's the one,
Knows all the tricks
That causes man,
To make bad picks.

<u>Eternal Security</u>

You can get back,
In God's good grace.
So when you die,
You forever, see His loving face.

Just choose to Him obey
For He sacrificed His Son,
On that fateful Easter day,
Your race was finally won.

<u>Heaven. . . . . . .</u>

He'll find your name
Is written there.
From then, for ever after,
You're always in His care.

Written by oldbuck, In a feeble attempt to write yet another
Children's Bible Study rhyme.
I fear it is far too "heavy" for most kids.

RHYME 41
Wherein "Lies" the Answer?

As I set here at the keyboard,
And think of things, today I saw.
It reminds me now of something
I'm roughly Quoting: Bernard Shaw.

"You surely must know someone,
There may be 5 or 6.
That if you set them down, and asked:
My friend what makes you tick?"

"As you set there. . . . . .think real hard,
Just how have you helped out?
We're asking you today to tell,
There is no time to whine or pout?"

"Have the things that you've accomplished,
Made 'you worth 'what you have cost?
We're running out of "green" resources,
Must remember when they're lost."

"There is no magic money tree,
That keeps us well supplied.
If you're not doing all you can,
It may be time you died."

"It may sound so very harsh,
As we're now asking you.
But science has come up,
With their solution too."

"There is a painless,
Yet efficient gas.
One long, deep, whiff,
This moment too. . . shall pass."

"I didn't say with one long whiff,
You'd suddenly pass gas.
I'm really saying, here so gently,
Your life, will soon be past."

"End of paraphrased quote."

I can imagine what you're thinking,
Where do these notions start?
When we seek answers near the end,
Each one must do their part.

We've asked our government workers,
To take some minor cuts.
The Union Bosses looked at us,
And said: " You really must be nuts ! "

We went then to the schools,
Their budgets seem to grow.
They were amazed that we could ask,
With those little tykes all in a row.

We went to Nations, near and far,
And suggested we'd make cuts.
They can't live without our help,
They're living in 'hand-out' ruts.

There are those poor and needy,
Some living under concrete piers.
How can we now, cut off the funds,
And starve these innocent dears.

Of course there are those "elders",
Some seem to live near poverty.
They've all paid, long in advance,
Now simply state, "Just leave us be."

Some said:" the Pentagon's our mark,"
It's our budget, near a fourth.
But even we, with hardened heart,
Can't short the U.S. Force.

Of course the Politician's,
They could all afford to give.
But here again the laws are such,
That they may "privileged" live.

Here my friend is where we're at,
So everyone must sooner die.
So we can keep on, keeping on,
Living as always. . .Some too high.

But as you read tomorrows news,
In days to come, when the shoe fits.
Remember this, <u>the answers plain.</u>
It will come down to this. . . .
"You're it."

Written by oldbuck, after hearing: An independent group of
doctors, nurses, medical experts and consumers may look at all
the evidence and recommend the best ways to reduce
unnecessary spending.

It may have put him in a rather dark and pensive mood, as
Thomas Paine may have been, when he wrote in 1776 :

"The American Crisis".
"These are the times that try men's souls."
*Some will, in this crisis, shrink from the service of their
country; but he that stands by it now, deserves the love &
thanks of all American's.*

Until we meet again.

Here in this brass urn,
Are just ashes and bone.
But I've added my prayers,
He'll not go alone.

I fear my prayers are now ignored,
As he nears the "Golden" gate.
If he's made no prior decision,
I suspect it's far too late.

But I feel I should say them
He was not a "bad" guy.
I certainly wouldn't want him,
For all eternity to fry.

In the years that I knew him,
As a friend. . . . more a chum.
He was seldom then lazy
Nor lived as a bum.

He loved to bring smiles,
On folks sad or sullen faces.
Often voicing weird comments,
In the oddest of places.

There's one thing I know
Has now given relief.
When we spoke of Jesus
He oft shared his "Belief."

For that's all that matters,
To then get inside.
For it is only Believers,
With "Him" will reside.

So if as you read this,
You've given it thought.
And ask if your "goodness",
A "mansion" has bought.

You've read it here now,
But it's always been so.
Without Faith in Jesus,
It's to hell you must go.

But "You" still have time,
Set your pride aside.
Tell Jesus you trust Him,
Want to be now His "bride".

Written by oldbuck,
As he thought of friends who've gone on ahead.
How many had he failed to tell because it
might have affected their relationship.
* * * * * * * * * *
I've handed out a few copies of it, with this request.
If they attend my funeral, I would like them to read this.
I've made my family agree, there will be a good luncheon.

A Note to those that have read this far:
This is my second book of rhymes.
I started them both with the same rhyme.
It was my first and I have always thought, my best.
I close this book with another from the first book.
It pretty well sums up any "important" thoughts.

Made in the USA
Middletown, DE
11 June 2019